My United States

Maine

ROBIN S. DOAK

Children's Press®
An Imprint of Scholastic Inc.

Content Consultant

James Wolfinger, PhD, Associate Dean and Professor
College of Education, DePaul University, Chicago, Illinois

Library of Congress Cataloging-in-Publication Data
Names: Doak, Robin S. (Robin Santos), 1963- author.
Title: Maine / by Robin Doak.
Description: New York : Children's Press, an imprint of Scholastic Inc., 2018. | Series: A true book | Includes
    bibliographical references and index.
Identifiers: LCCN 2017025786 | ISBN 9780531231661 (library binding) | ISBN 9780531247174 (pbk.)
Subjects: LCSH: Maine—Juvenile literature.
Classification: LCC F19.3 .D63 2018 | DDC 974.1—dc23
LC record available at https://lccn.loc.gov/2017025786

All rights reserved. Published in 2018 by Children's Press, an imprint of Scholastic Inc.
Printed in North Mankato, MN, USA 113

SCHOLASTIC, CHILDREN'S PRESS, A TRUE BOOK™, and associated logos are trademarks and/or registered trademarks of
Scholastic Inc.

Scholastic Inc., 557 Broadway, New York, NY 10012

1 2 3 4 5 6 7 8 9 10 R 27 26 25 24 23 22 21 20 19 18

Front cover: Bass Harbor Head Lighthouse

Back cover: A lobster

Welcome to Maine

Key Facts

Capital: Augusta

Estimated population as of 2016: 1,331,479

Nickname: The Pine Tree State

Biggest cities: Portland, Lewiston, Bangor

Find the Truth!

Everything you are about to read is true *except* for one of the sentences on this page.

Which one is **TRUE**?

T or F Maine is home to the northernmost end of the Appalachian Trail.

T or F Maine was the last of the original 13 colonies to be formed.

Find the answers in this book.

Contents

THE **BIG** TRUTH!

Blueberries

What Represents Maine?

Lobster

Hiking on Bald Mountain

Maine
Coon cat

This Is Maine!

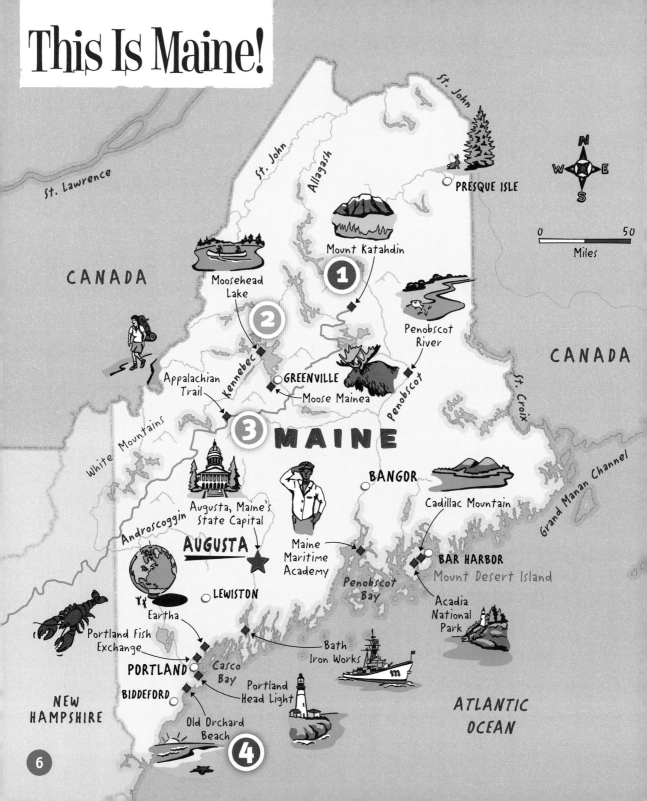

St. Lawrence

St. John

St. John

Allagash

PRESQUE ISLE

Mount Katahdin

1

CANADA

Moosehead Lake

2

Penobscot River

CANADA

Appalachian Trail

Kennebec

GREENVILLE

Moose Mainea

Penobscot

St. Croix

3 MAINE

White Mountains

Augusta, Maine's State Capital

BANGOR

Cadillac Mountain

Grand Manan Channel

AUGUSTA

Maine Maritime Academy

Androscoggin

Penobscot Bay

BAR HARBOR
Mount Desert Island

Acadia National Park

LEWISTON

Eartha

Portland Fish Exchange

PORTLAND

Casco Bay

Bath Iron Works

PORTLAND

BIDDEFORD

Portland Head Light

NEW HAMPSHIRE

Old Orchard Beach

4

ATLANTIC OCEAN

N W E S

0   50
Miles

① Mount Katahdin

Maine's tallest peak is a popular spot for hiking and camping. Visitors can enjoy beautiful views and get a glimpse at local wildlife.

② Moosehead Lake

Maine's biggest lake is so large that it contains more than 80 islands. This popular tourist destination has some of the state's most lovely scenery.

③ Appalachian Trail

This 2,200-mile (3,541-kilometer) trail begins at Mount Katahdin and heads south through the Appalachian Mountains all the way to Georgia. As one of the world's longest hiking trails, it draws visitors from all around the globe.

④ Old Orchard Beach

Visit this popular destination to enjoy Maine's coastal beaches during the summer. You can go swimming or boating, or just enjoy the view.

There are more than 60 lighthouses along Maine's coast.

CHAPTER 1

Land and Wildlife

Located on the East Coast of the United States, Maine is famous for its wild, untamed scenery. Rocky, windswept beaches line the coast. Lush green forests, crystal-clear lakes, and rushing rivers dot the inner regions. Maine is the largest state in the area known as New England. The state is home to 1.3 million people, but millions more visit each year to enjoy Maine's beauty. This state has everything to offer to those who love the outdoors!

Outdoor Paradise

Maine is bordered by Canada to the northwest and northeast and New Hampshire to the southwest. Its southeastern border is the Atlantic Ocean. Its coastline is mostly rough and rocky, but there are also some smooth, sandy beaches. More than 4,000 islands dot the coastline. Moving inland, Maine's central region has thick forests, tall mountains, and deep freshwater lakes.

This map shows where the higher (red and orange) and lower (green) areas are in Maine.

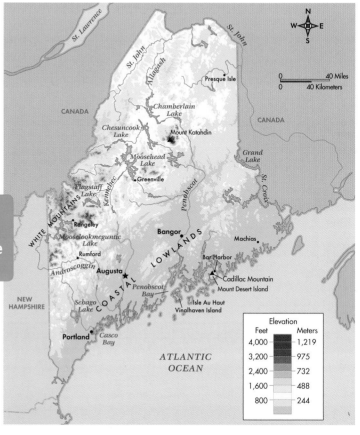

Acadia National Park

Acadia National Park is located on Maine's Mount Desert Island and the surrounding area. It is New England's only national park. Visitors come to the park for its breathtaking views of the Atlantic Ocean. They also hike or bike along its many trails, hoping to catch a glimpse of its native wildlife species. With more than 40 miles (64 km) of coastline and 47,700 acres (19,303 hectares) of land, it has plenty of places to explore. One park attraction is Thunder Hole, a small cavern just under the ocean's surface. Wind and waves create spectacular sprays of water and thundering noises here.

A Rocky Peak

The Appalachian Mountains cut their way through the northwestern part of the state. The highest point in Maine, Mount Katahdin, is here. Katahdin measures 5,267 feet (1,605 meters) from top to bottom. It is the northern end of the Appalachian Trail. With its sheer cliff faces and rocky ledges, Katahdin can be a challenge for even the best climbers to hike.

Mount Katahdin is located in Baxter State Park.

Baxter State Park is named for the governor who bought and donated the park's land.

MAXIMUM TEMPERATURE 105°F MINIMUM TEMPERATURE -50°F

Visitors flock to Acadia National Park and other places across Maine to see autumn colors.

Climate

Maine has a **temperate** climate. There are four distinct seasons to each year. Winters are cold and snowy. The northern part of the state receives an average snowfall of up to 110 inches (279 centimeters). Southern and coastal areas are less severe. Summers in the state are warm and comfortable. Temperatures average 70 degrees Fahrenheit (21 degrees Celsius). Spring and fall are also mild and comfortable. Maine's fall **foliage** attracts visitors from around the world.

Lady's slippers are a type of orchid native to the Northeast.

Forests and Flowers

Forests make up about 90 percent of Maine's land. Most of these wooded areas are softwood forests in the north. Softwood trees include spruce, fir, and pine. Hardwood forests—filled with maple, oak, and birch—can be found in the south. Maine also has many types of flowers, including several rare orchid **species**. The state is famous for its wild blueberry bushes.

Moose and More

Maine's forests are home to a variety of wildlife. Hikers might spot moose, black bears, white-tailed deer, bobcats, foxes, beavers, and many other animals. Some of Maine's nearly 300 types of birds include bald eagles, ospreys, owls, and loons. Puffins live along the coast. Sea creatures flourish in Maine's cold coastal waters, from lobsters and clams to seals and porpoises. Maine is also home to amphibians and reptiles, including salamanders, turtles, and nonvenomous snakes.

Male moose shed their antlers and grow new ones each year.

Charles Bulfinch, who designed the U.S. Capitol in Washington, D.C., also designed Maine's capitol.

CHAPTER 2

Government

When Maine became a state in 1820, Portland was its capital. Portland was Maine's largest city, but it is far to the south. Many Mainers felt the capital should be in a more central location. In 1827, lawmakers chose the city of Augusta. Five years later, the state legislature met in the newly built capitol there for the first time. Although Portland tried several times to become the capital again, Augusta remains Maine's government center.

State Government Basics

Maine's constitution, adopted in 1820, created the state's government. The government is made up of three equal branches. The executive branch, headed by the governor, is responsible for enforcing the state's laws. The legislative branch, which is the Senate and the House of Representatives, makes the state's laws. The judicial branch, made up of the state's courts, interprets these laws.

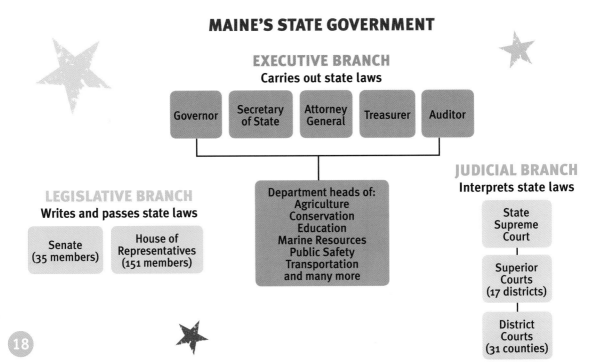

MAINE'S STATE GOVERNMENT

EXECUTIVE BRANCH
Carries out state laws

| Governor | Secretary of State | Attorney General | Treasurer | Auditor |

LEGISLATIVE BRANCH
Writes and passes state laws

| Senate (35 members) | House of Representatives (151 members) |

Department heads of:
Agriculture
Conservation
Education
Marine Resources
Public Safety
Transportation
and many more

JUDICIAL BRANCH
Interprets state laws

State Supreme Court

Superior Courts (17 districts)

District Courts (31 counties)

A larger portion of Maine's population shows up to vote than in many other states.

Voter Power

Voters in Maine have the power to recommend and vote on new laws. Proposed laws cannot violate the state constitution. In 2016, voters passed four new laws crafted by Maine's citizens. For example, one of the laws promises to increase the state's minimum wage over time. The laws went into effect in 2017. In Maine, the governor has no power to **veto** this type of law. However, legislators may **amend** these laws in the future.

Maine in the National Government

Each state elects officials to represent it in the U.S. Congress. Like every other state, Maine has two senators. The U.S. House of Representatives relies on a state's population to determine its numbers. Maine has two representatives in the House.

Every four years, states vote on the next U.S. president. Each state is granted a number of electoral votes based on its number of members in Congress. Maine has four. Unlike most states, Maine can split its votes between presidential candidates.

2 senators and 4 representatives

4 electoral votes

With four electoral votes, Maine's voice in presidential elections is below average compared to other states.

Representing Maine

Elected officials in Maine represent a population
with a range of interests, lifestyles, and backgrounds.

Ethnicity (2016 estimates)

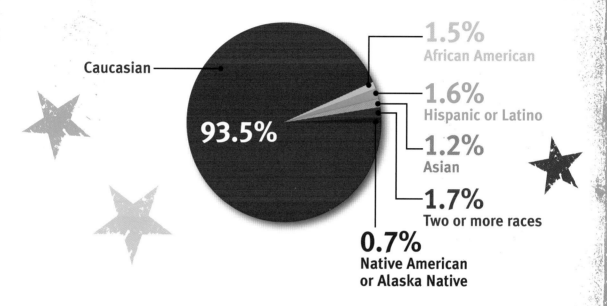

Caucasian

93.5%

1.5%
African American

1.6%
Hispanic or Latino

1.2%
Asian

1.7%
Two or more races

0.7%
Native American
or Alaska Native

3.5% of Mainers were born in other countries.

71% own their own homes.

There are about **119,000** military veterans.

92% of the population graduated from high school.

29% of the population have a degree beyond high school.

70% live in cities.

21

What Represents Maine?

States choose specific animals, plants, and objects to represent the values and characteristics of the land and its people. Find out why these symbols were chosen to represent Maine or discover surprising curiosities about them.

Seal

The man on the left is a farmer. The one on the right is a sailor. In the center is a pine tree with a moose lying beneath it. At the top of the seal is the North Star. Below that is the word *Dirigo*, which is Latin for "I lead."

Flag

Maine's flag, bearing the state seal, was adopted by lawmakers in 1909.

Lobster

STATE CRUSTACEAN

A lobster's teeth are in its stomach, where they grind up the lobster's meal.

Honeybee

STATE INSECT

A small hive can include 20,000 of these insects.

Whoopie Pie

STATE TREAT

This sweet treat has been enjoyed in Maine since the 1920s.

Maine Coon

STATE CAT

These cats are among the largest domestic, or pet, cats in the world.

Moxie

STATE SOFT DRINK

Lisbon, Maine, holds an annual Moxie Festival celebrating this sweet and somewhat bitter soft drink.

Wild Blueberry

STATE BERRY

Though these berries can grow wild, they are also often farmed and harvested. In fact, wild blueberry crops are a large part of the state's income.

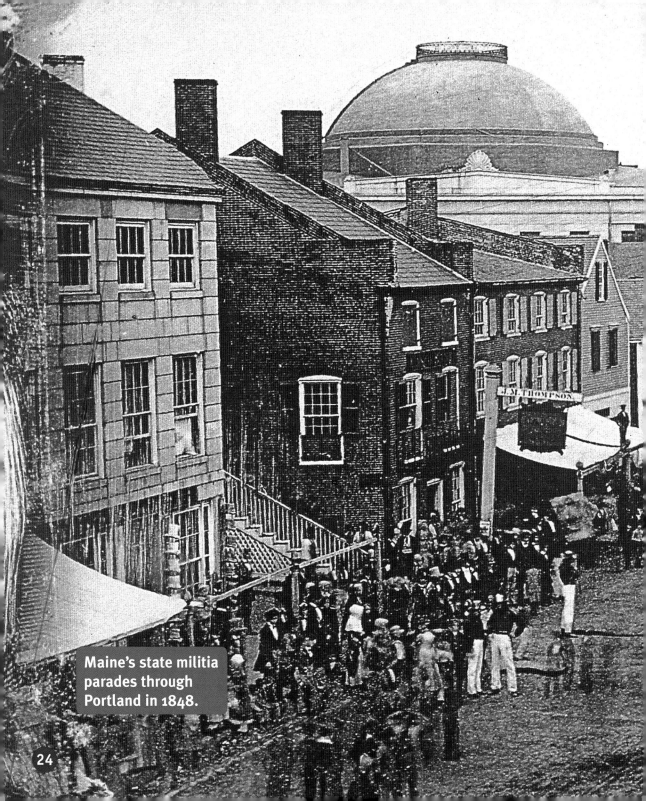

Maine's state militia parades through Portland in 1848.

History

Maine's history is thousands of years old. The first people to live in the region migrated there about 11,000 years ago. In 1000 CE, Vikings may have sailed to the area from Iceland looking for good fishing grounds. Other groups of people followed in later years.

The name Mayne was first used in 1622, but no one is quite sure why. It may have come from early explorers, who called the area the Main, short for "mainland."

Native Americans

The first people to live in Maine were Paleo-Indians more than 11,000 years ago. Later, other tribes settled in the area. They included the Maliseet, Passamaquoddy, Abenaki, and Penobscot. These peoples shared a similar language and way of life. They built birchbark canoes to fish in coastal waters and lakes. They hunted in Maine's forests, and planted beans, corn, and squash for food.

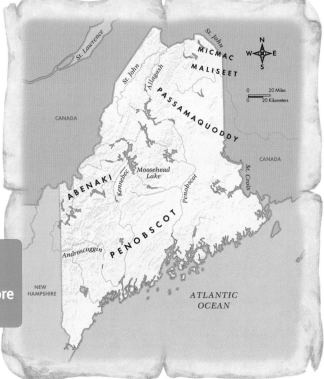

This map shows some of the major tribes that lived in what is now Maine before Europeans came.

Despite disease and foreign invasion, the Penobscots, Passamaquoddys, and other tribes survived into the 20th century and beyond.

Life changed in the 1500s with the arrival of Europeans from France, Italy, and other countries. These explorers brought diseases such as **smallpox** to the area. The diseases killed three out of every four native people in Maine. To survive, the tribes banded together with the Micmac people to the north. They formed the Wabanaki Confederacy to protect themselves and their land from white settlers and native enemy groups.

European Exploration

When European explorers arrived in the 1500s, they charted the coastline. They found that the area was rich in natural resources such as fish, animals with valuable fur, and lumber. The British first tried to settle Maine in 1607, but the bitter winters drove them away. When they tried again in 1630, the settlers were more successful.

This map shows routes European explorers took as they explored and settled what is now Maine.

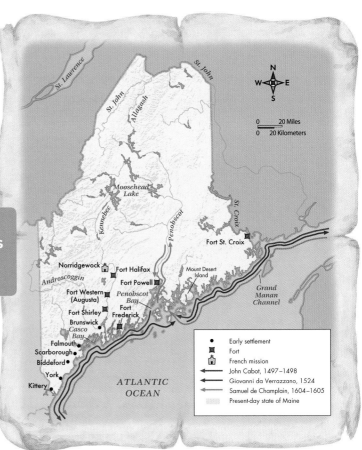

British colonial troops fight Native Americans who had sided with France in the French and Indian War.

In 1652, Maine was combined with the British colony of Massachusetts. Maine became the site of multiple battles after the French and Indian War began in 1754. This war between France and Great Britain was over who owned areas of North America, including Maine. Native American groups also fought on both sides of the war. In 1763, Great Britain defeated France, and more British and other settlers began making Maine their permanent home.

Road to Statehood

During the American Revolution (1775–1783), many Mainers fought for independence from Great Britain. When the United States won, soldiers were given land in Maine. By the early 1800s, Mainers began pushing to split from Massachusetts. In 1820, a law added Maine and Missouri as the 23rd and 24th states. The law made Missouri a slave state and Maine a free, non-slave state.

Timeline of Maine Events

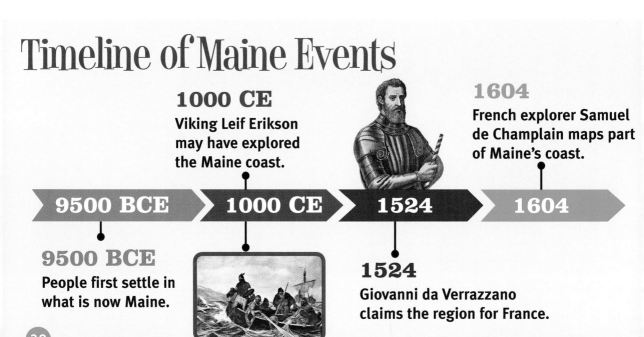

1000 CE
Viking Leif Erikson may have explored the Maine coast.

1604
French explorer Samuel de Champlain maps part of Maine's coast.

9500 BCE · **1000 CE** · **1524** · **1604**

9500 BCE
People first settle in what is now Maine.

1524
Giovanni da Verrazzano claims the region for France.

Modern Maine

During the Civil War (1861–1865), nearly 73,000 Mainers joined the Union Army. They fought the Confederacy, 11 Southern states that had left the country and wanted to keep slavery legal.

After the war, many **industries** took root in Maine. Paper mills and a steel shipbuilding yard in Bath boosted the state's economy. Still, most Mainers farmed for a living.

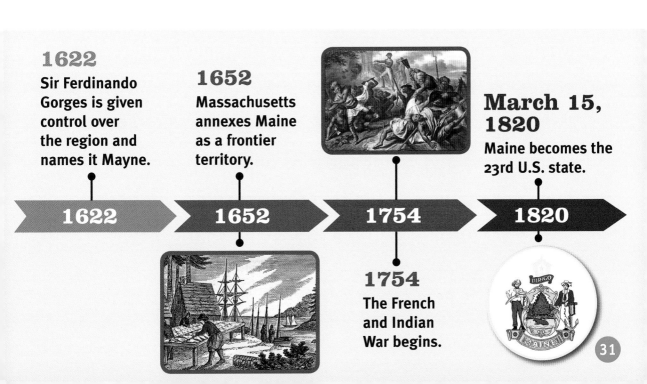

1622
Sir Ferdinando Gorges is given control over the region and names it Mayne.

1652
Massachusetts annexes Maine as a frontier territory.

March 15, 1820
Maine becomes the 23rd U.S. state.

1622 — 1652 — 1754 — 1820

1754
The French and Indian War begins.

Farmers wait outside a factory to deliver their potatoes.

Like the rest of the country, Maine's economy was hurt by the Great Depression in the 1930s. Many Mainers suffered as the national economy struggled. World War II (1939–1945) saw a boom in industry in the state and across the United States. Maine's tree and water supplies allowed paper and power companies to flourish. Tourism was another important business. In the 1970s and 1980s, new highways and businesses attracted thousands of new residents.

Paving the Way

In June 1940, Maine voters elected Margaret Chase Smith (1897–1995) to the U.S. House of Representatives. During her 30-year career in politics, Smith fought for women's rights and other issues. In 1948, she was elected to the U.S. Senate, becoming the first woman to serve in both houses of Congress. In 1964, she ran for the Republican **nomination** for president. Smith lost, but she inspired a high school student: Hillary Rodham, later presidential nominee Hillary Rodham Clinton.

33

Cross-country skiing is a popular activity in the woods of Maine.

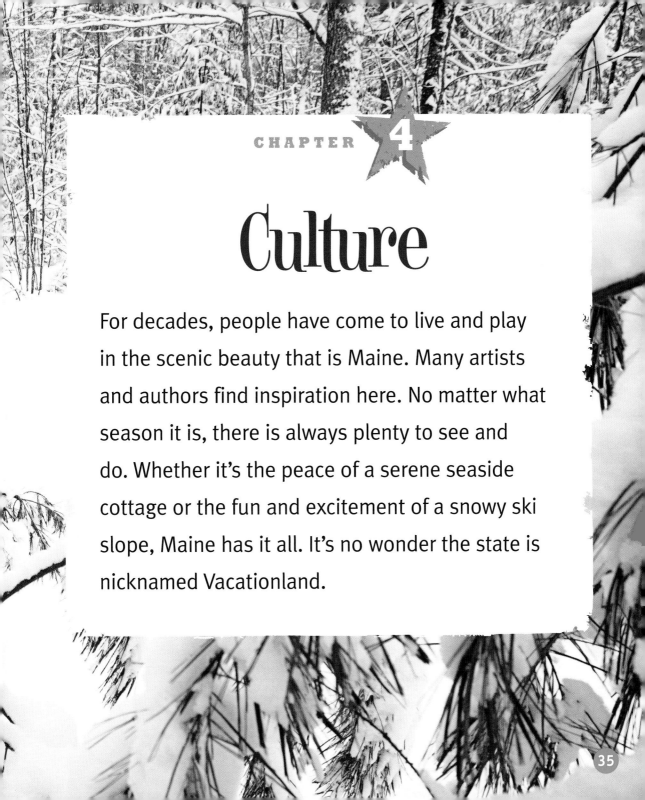

CHAPTER 4

Culture

For decades, people have come to live and play in the scenic beauty that is Maine. Many artists and authors find inspiration here. No matter what season it is, there is always plenty to see and do. Whether it's the peace of a serene seaside cottage or the fun and excitement of a snowy ski slope, Maine has it all. It's no wonder the state is nicknamed Vacationland.

Canoeing through white water is a challenging activity some Mainers enjoy.

Maine at Play

Maine has no professional sports team, but that doesn't mean Mainers don't enjoy sports. The state has many public parks and wildlife protection areas. They include sandy beaches to walk along and high mountains to climb or ski. Boaters can visit the Allagash Wilderness Waterway. At Portland Head Light, visitors can fly a kite, then eat a lobster lunch at a nearby restaurant. In the north, fishers, hunters, and snowmobilers enjoy Maine at its wildest.

Celebrating Maine Style

Maine's long heritage of farms and farming is celebrated in the many agricultural fairs each year. The largest of these is the Fryeburg Fair. The Skowhegan State Fair has been held every year since 1818. It is one of the nation's oldest. The largest single-day event in Maine is the Old Port Festival in Portland. For more than 40 years, people have enjoyed music, food, crafts, and entertainment at this summer funfest.

A competitor takes part in a bucksawing competition at the annual fair in Fryeburg.

Off to Work

Maine still has many farmers and fishers. Some Maine crops include potatoes, wild blueberries, and apples. Maine lobsters are shipped around the world, as are softshell clams, sea urchins, cod, and other fish. There are currently about 6,000 lobster fishers in Maine. Each person can fish up to 800 traps at one time. Other industries that are important to Maine include health care, tourism, and retail such as shops. Education and construction also add jobs for Maine residents.

On average, Maine farmers are younger than those in many other states.

A Fishing Heritage

While technology has changed many industries in Maine, lobster fishing has remained mostly unchanged. Several small fishing villages lie along the Atlantic coast. Here, men and women still use traps very similar to ones used 200 years ago. The lobster fishers put bait into the traps, then throw the traps overboard. The traps are each marked with a specially colored **buoy** to help the fishers find them again.

Maine fishers brought in more than 130 million pounds (59 million kilograms) of lobster in 2016.

On the Table

The clambake is a Maine food tradition. Native Americans may have introduced white settlers to clambakes in the 1600s. A true clambake is held on the beach. Lobsters, corn, clams, and potatoes are cooked slowly over a fire made of driftwood and seaweed. Dessert might include blueberry pie or whoopie pies.

 ## Maine Lobster Roll

Ask an adult to help you!

Ingredients
1 cup chunked lobster meat
1 celery stalk, chopped
3 tablespoons mayonnaise
Salt and pepper to taste
1 tablespoon unsalted butter
2 top-split hot dog buns (or bun of your choice)

Directions
Combine lobster, celery, mayonnaise, and salt and pepper in a bowl. Cover the bowl with plastic wrap and refrigerate for up to 30 minutes. Spread butter on the outside of the buns. With an adult's help, toast the buns in a frying pan until they are golden brown. Spoon the lobster mix into the buns and enjoy!

The Way Life Should Be

Beautiful scenery, outdoor adventures, friendly people, fantastic food—Maine is all this and much more. Those who visit Maine quickly learn why the state is so special. In fact, most Maine visitors are repeat tourists. They come back again and again to enjoy all that the state offers. Mainers take pride in their state's history, heritage, and traditions. Ask Mainers if their state is a great place to be. They'll tell you, "Ayuh!" ★

Famous People

Henry Wadsworth Longfellow

(1807–1882) was a famous poet and author who was born in Portland. Tourists can visit his childhood home.

Harriet Beecher Stowe

(1811–1896) was a writer who opposed slavery. She wrote *Uncle Tom's Cabin*, an important anti-slavery book, at Bowdoin College in Brunswick.

Robert E. Peary

(1856–1920) was an explorer who made several trips to the Arctic. In 1906, he claimed to be the first man to reach the North Pole. He grew up in Portland.

Percy Spencer

(1894–1970) was a scientist who invented the microwave oven. Born and raised in Howland, he was inducted into the National Inventors Hall of Fame in 1999.

E. B. White

(1899–1985) was a writer. He owned a summer home in Brooklin that served as the inspiration for his book *Charlotte's Web*. He also wrote the classic children's novel *Stuart Little*.

Andrew Wyeth

(1917–2009) was a painter who spent his summers in Cushing. His most famous work, *Christina's World*, was painted in Maine.

George H. W. Bush

(1924–) was the 41st president of the United States. He and his family spend summers at their home in Kennebunkport.

Stephen King

(1947–) is a best-selling author of horror stories, including *It* and *The Shining*. Many of his books have been turned into movies. He was raised in Maine and has a home in Bangor.

Joan Benoit Samuelson

(1957–) is a marathon runner who won a gold medal at the 1984 Olympic Games. She has set a number of marathon records. She lives in Freeport.

Anna Kendrick

(1985–) is an actress who has appeared in many movies. She is the voice of Poppy in the animated film *Trolls*. In 2010, she was nominated for an Oscar. She was born and raised in Portland.

Did You Know That ...

The Desert of Maine is in Freeport. The land here became sandy and barren after years of farming. Today it is a tourist attraction.

Earmuffs were invented by 15-year-old Chester Greenwood of Farmington in 1873. He needed something to protect his ears while ice-skating.

Each year, people at the annual Maine Lobster Festival in Rockland eat up to 25,000 pounds (11,340 kg) of lobster.

Maine is larger in size than all the other New England states combined.

L.L. Bean began making Bean Boots in 1912. His company continues that tradition today.

The East Coast Greenway is a planned bike trail that will be 3,000 miles (4,828 km) long. When it is complete, it will stretch from Calais, Maine, to Key West, Florida.

B&M Baked Beans originated in Portland, Maine. The beans are still cooked in open pots inside brick ovens.

Milton Bradley, the inventor of the game known today as Life, was born in Vienna.

As many as 70,000 moose live in Maine.

Did you find the truth?

T Maine is home to the northernmost end of the Appalachian Trail.

F Maine was the last of the original 13 colonies to be formed.

Resources

Books

Nonfiction

Goodridge, Harry. *A Seal Called Andre*. Camden, ME: Down East Books, 2014.

Gregory, Josh. *Moose*. New York: Children's Press, 2016.

Heinrichs, Ann. *Maine*. New York: Children's Press, 2014.

Wallace, Audra. *Acadia*. New York: Children's Press, 2018.

Fiction

Blume, Judy. *Fudge-a-mania*. New York: Dutton Children's Books, 1990.

Schmidt, Gary D. *Lizzie Bright and the Buckminster Boy*. New York: Clarion Books, 2004.

Visit this Scholastic website for more information on Maine:

★ www.factsfornow.scholastic.com
Enter the keyword **Maine**

Important Words

amend (uh-MEND) to change a legal document or a law

buoy (BOO-ee) a floating marker, often with a bell or a light

foliage (FOH-lee-ij) the leaves of a plant or tree

industries (IN-duh-streez) branches of business or trade

nomination (nah-muh-NAY-shuhn) the formal process of putting someone forward as a candidate for an important job, such as president

smallpox (SMAWL-poks) a very contagious, or easily spread, disease that causes a rash, high fever, and blisters that can leave permanent scars

species (SPEE-sheez) groups of animals or plants that can produce offspring

temperate (TEM-pur-it) describing an area where temperatures are rarely very high or very low

veto (VEE-toh) to forbid something, or to stop a bill from becoming a law

Index

Page numbers in **bold** indicate illustrations.

About the Author

Robin S. Doak has a bachelor's degree in English from the University of Connecticut. She currently lives with her husband in a small Maine town. She has been writing for children for nearly 30 years.